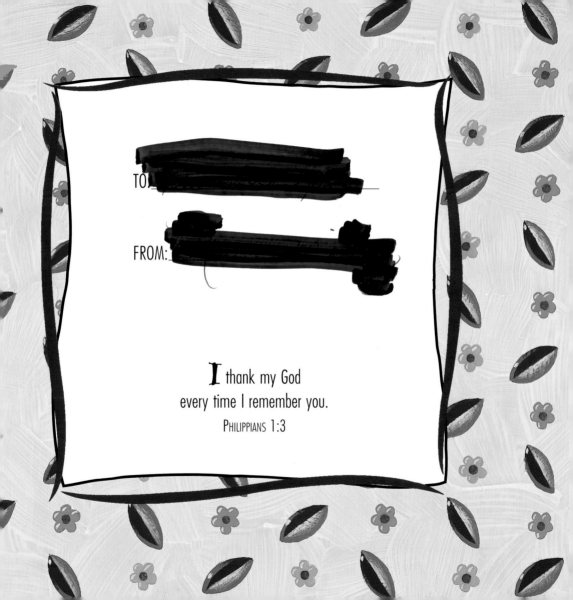

TO:

FROM:

I thank my God
every time I remember you.
PHILIPPIANS 1:3

Requests for information should be addressed to:
ZondervanPublishingHouse
5300 Patterson S.E. • Grand Rapids, MI 49530
http://www.zondervan.com

Editorial Director: Joy Marple
Project Editor: Conover Swofford
Production Editor: Pat Matuszak
Graphic Design: Robin Welsh
Illustrations: Erika LeBarre

Printed in China
97 98 99 / HK / 3 2 1

YOUR **FRIENDSHIP**

IS **HEAVEN** SENT

Let us love one another, for love comes from God.

1 JOHN 4:7

Do not forsake your friend.

Proverbs 27:10

_____

Father,
Thank you for this special friend who loves me
and whom I love. Thank you for the bond
between us. Bless her and bless our friendship.

Amen

I always thank my God
as I remember you in my prayers.
Your love has given me
great joy and encouragement.

Philemon 4, 7

Do two walk together unless they
have agreed to do so?

Amos 3:3

A friend is someone who sees the visions
of your mind as worthy and beautiful
and manages to keep a straight face
while she does so.

Every good and perfect gift is from above,
coming down from the Father of the heavenly lights,
who does not change like shifting shadows.

JAMES 1:17

After the friendship of God,
a friend's affection
is the greatest treasure below.

ANONYMOUS

It's a mystery how two imperfect people
can have one perfect friendship,
but with God's help we've managed
to do just that.

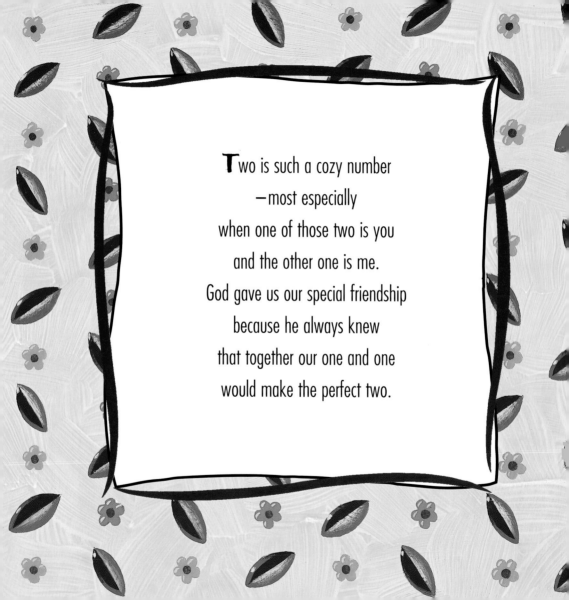

Two is such a cozy number
—most especially
when one of those two is you
and the other one is me.
God gave us our special friendship
because he always knew
that together our one and one
would make the perfect two.

Two are better than one.

ECCLESIASTES 4:9

Two hearts that share laughter and pain.
Two souls that share a faith.
Two minds that help each other grow.
I'm glad God made us friends.

*W*hen I needed a friend,

God answered my prayers

and sent you to me.

The greatest gift from God

is a true friend like you.

A friend loves at all times.

PROVERBS 17:17

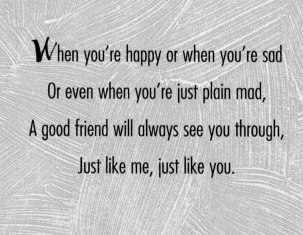

When you're happy or when you're sad
Or even when you're just plain mad,
A good friend will always see you through,
Just like me, just like you.

A friend is

someone to whom you can talk forever

and still find things to say,

but who doesn't always need words

to know how you feel.

*C*arry each other's burdens
and in this way you will fulfill the law of Christ.

GALATIANS 6:2

I greatly appreciate the way you keep
my confidences. How wonderful to have a friend
I can tell anything to!

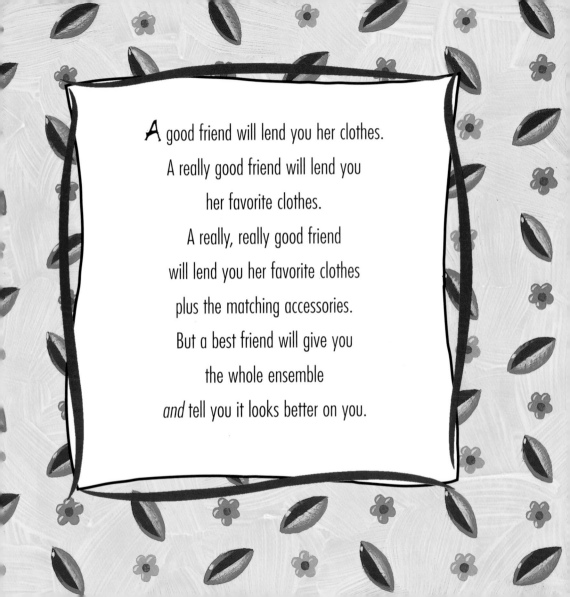

A good friend will lend you her clothes.
A really good friend will lend you
her favorite clothes.
A really, really good friend
will lend you her favorite clothes
plus the matching accessories.
But a best friend will give you
the whole ensemble
and tell you it looks better on you.

A friend is someone who always remembers your birthday
but never your age.

We're not always perfect,

But we try to be good.

We try to help each other

Do the things we should.

Sometimes our "straight and narrow"

May get a little bent.

We may not be angelic

But our friendship's heaven sent.

Whenever I need a little boost

over the bumps of life,

you're always right there.

I cannot imagine

how I would cope with life

without you (and caffeine)!

What is a friend?
A single soul
dwelling in two bodies.

ARISTOTLE

A friend is someone
who is interested
in the same things you are—
your life, your job,
your family, your ideas.

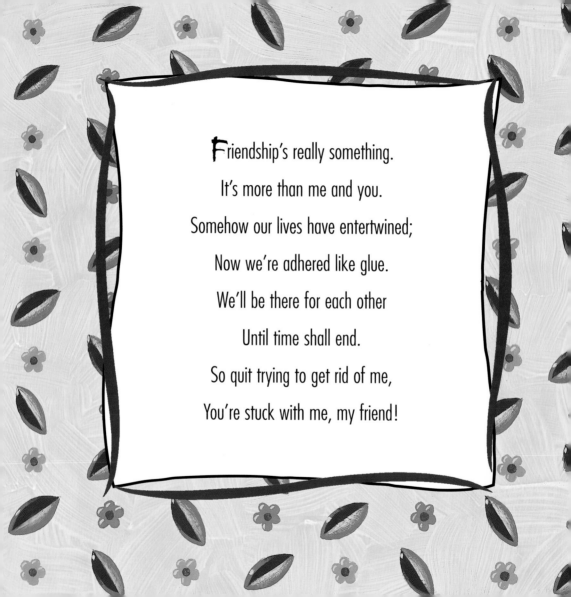

Friendship's really something.

It's more than me and you.

Somehow our lives have entertwined;

Now we're adhered like glue.

We'll be there for each other

Until time shall end.

So quit trying to get rid of me,

You're stuck with me, my friend!

Nothing but Heaven itself
is better than a friend who is really a friend.

Titus Maccius Plautus

My friend,
I want your life to be as beautiful
as it was in the mind of God
when he first thought of you.

Anonymous

You are such a good friend
that I know if I had any faults,
you would simply remind me and others
that flaws make me more interesting
than boring perfection.

Wounds from a friend can be trusted.

PROVERBS 27:6

I'm thankful that

you care enough about me

to be the speedbump

that slows me down

whenever I am trying to

run ahead of God.

Above all,
love each other deeply,
because love covers
over a multitude of sins.

1 PETER 4:8

I appreciate the loving way
you polish up my rough spots
without rubbing me the wrong way.

Have you ever wondered
if God made us friends because
we truly appreciate each other
or because we are,
perhaps, too unique for other people
to truly appreciate?

And my God
will meet all your needs.

PHILIPPIANS 4:19

God knew we each needed
a special friend,
so he arranged our lives to coincide.

A cheerful heart is good medicine.

PROVERBS 17:22

You know I always pray for you
and when I do,
I thank God continually for all the things
you mean to me.

~~~~~~~~~~~~

You are a much better pain reliever
than aspirin could ever be.

We have our own unique style,

Joint memories we recall;

And whenever we're together,

A good time is had by all.

My friend,
I pray God's special blessing
upon you today.
May he give you something wonderful
to make your day a joyful one,
just as you're a joy to me.
May he bless you
as your friendship has blessed me.

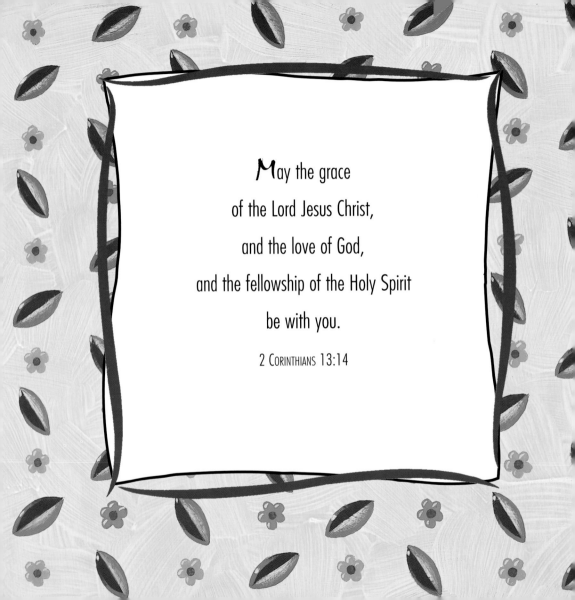

May the grace
of the Lord Jesus Christ,
and the love of God,
and the fellowship of the Holy Spirit
be with you.

2 Corinthians 13:14

A friend is someone who shares with you

a smile, a tear, a hand.

A friend is someone who cares for you;

a heart that can understand.

A friend is someone you can just be with,

even when there's nothing to do.

A friend is someone you can laugh with;

I'm glad my friend is you.

Friend, pal, comrade, crony, chum

Who looks the other way

when I do something dumb;

I wish you'd do something silly, too,

So I could look the other way for you.

When I look at you, I not only see the reflection of myself as you see me,
but also the reflection of God's love as he pours it through you to me.

We love because he first loved us.

1 JOHN 4:19

As I have loved you,
so you must love one another.

JOHN 13:34

Friendship, gift of Heaven,
delight of great souls.

VOLTAIRE

Blessed are they
who have the gift of making friends,
for it is one of God's best gifts.
It involves many things,
but above all, the power of going out of one's self,
and appreciating
whatever is noble and loving in another.

Thomas Hughes

Blessed are the peacemakers,

for they shall be called sons of God.

MATTHEW 5:9

In the midst of hectic times

When troubles just won't cease;

You, my friend, are always here

To remind me of God's peace.

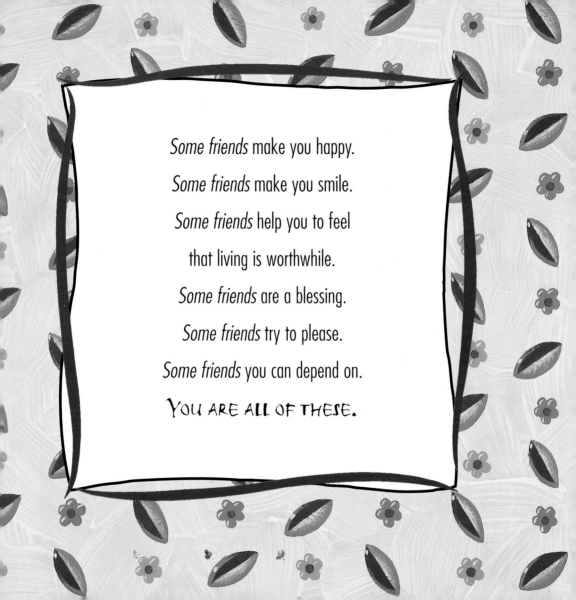

Some friends make you happy.

Some friends make you smile.

Some friends help you to feel

that living is worthwhile.

Some friends are a blessing.

Some friends try to please.

Some friends you can depend on.

YOU ARE ALL OF THESE.

A true friend is a true treasure.
You enrich my life.

A friend is the hope of the heart.

RALPH WALDO EMERSON

A friend is someone you can

go out with or stay in with

or just *be* with.

I know that we are friends
and nothing can keep us apart;
and thanks to God our Father
we're also sisters of the heart.

LAUGHTER.
The joy of sharing
the same sense of humor.

KNOWLEDGE.
Separate and shared.
Yours, mine, ours.

SUPPORT.
Always there when needed
to back each other up.

FRIENDSHIP.
One of God's best gifts.

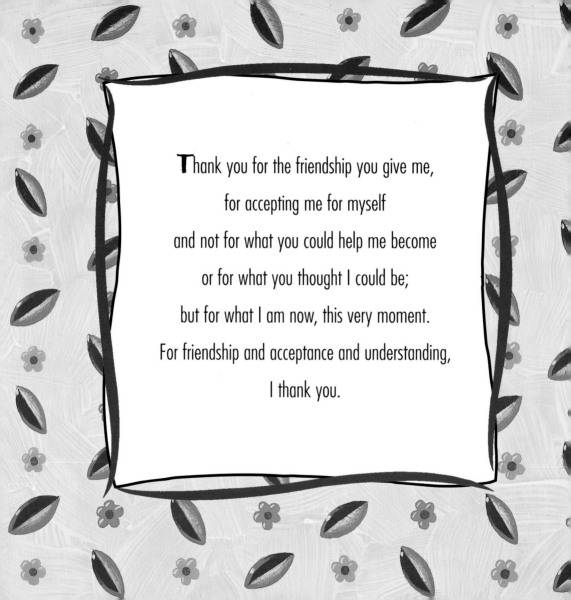

Thank you for the friendship you give me,

for accepting me for myself

and not for what you could help me become

or for what you thought I could be;

but for what I am now, this very moment.

For friendship and acceptance and understanding,

I thank you.

Father,

Thank you for the gift of friendship—

a heart to share joys and sorrows.

Thank you for this very special friend

and the love we share for each other and you.

Amen.

The LORD bless you and keep you;
the LORD make his face shine upon you
and be gracious to you;
the LORD turn his face toward you
and give you peace.

NUMBERS 6:24-26